# Margaret Bourke-White

by Catherine A. Welch
illustrations by Jennifer Hagerman

 Carolrhoda Books, Inc./Minneapolis

*To Amy Gelman, my editor*—C.A.W.

*To Heather and Rachel*—J.H.

The author wishes to thank Ingrid Davis and the staff of the Monroe (Connecticut) Public Library for their help in gathering material for this book. The events described in this book have been carefully researched. The primary sources were biographies and Margaret Bourke-White's writings (including autobiographical material). Quotations were taken from her work *Portrait of Myself.*

Text copyright © 1997 by Catherine A. Welch
Illustrations copyright © 1997 by Carolrhoda Books, Inc.

*This book is available in two editions:*
Library binding by Carolrhoda Books, Inc.
Soft cover by First Avenue Editions, 1997
c/o The Lerner Publishing Group
241 First Avenue North, Minneapolis, MN 55401 U.S.A.

Library of Congress Cataloging-in-Publication Data

Welch, Catherine A.
    Margaret Bourke-White / by Catherine A. Welch ; with
illustrations by Jennifer Hagerman.
        p.   cm. — (Carolrhoda on my own books)
    ISBN 0–87614–890–9 (lib. bdg.)
    ISBN 0–87614–956–5 (pbk.)
    1. Bourke-White, Margaret, 1904–1971—Juvenile literature.
    2. News photographers—United States—Biography—Juvenile literature.
    3. Women photographers—United States—Biography—
Juvenile literature. [1. Bourke-White, Margaret, 1904–1971.
    2. Photographers. 3. Women—Biography.] I. Hagerman, Jennifer,
ill. II. Title. III. Series: Carolrhoda on my own book.
    TR140.B6W45   1997
    770'.92—dc20
    [B]                                          95–11695

Manufactured in the United States of America
1  2  3  4  5  6  –  JR  –  02  01  00  99  98  97

# Author's Note

Margaret Bourke-White was born on June 14, 1904, at Harrison Avenue in the Bronx, New York City. She had an older sister, Ruth, and later, a younger brother, Roger. Minnie Bourke, her mother, was the daughter of an Irish ship's carpenter and an English cook. Joseph White, Margaret's father, was the son of Polish-Jewish immigrants.

Both Minnie and Joseph believed that doing your best was important. They were people eager to learn new things. Joseph was an engineer and inventor, working with printing presses. Minnie worked on books for the blind.

Margaret was born before radio, television, automobiles, and airplanes became part of everyday life. At that time, there were no picture magazines to bring news stories into people's homes. People read newspapers to learn about current events.

During Margaret's childhood, few working women had jobs that led them to adventures. Most were either teachers or secretaries.

But Margaret was not content to be like most women of her time. She wanted more. Her parents wanted more for her too.

Margaret looked at her mother, Minnie,
then glanced at the snake.
Minnie sat beside the fireplace
reading the Sunday newspaper.
She did not seem the least bit bothered
by the snake curled up in her lap.
The snake was Margaret's pet.
Margaret learned to enjoy snakes
while exploring the woods and hills
near the family's home
in Bound Brook, New Jersey.

As she hiked with her father, Joseph,
he pointed out the dangerous snakes.
He showed Margaret how to pick up
the harmless ones without being afraid.
Nature walks became adventures, and
Margaret began bringing snakes home.
Other creatures became
part of the family too.
One summer, Margaret raised
two hundred caterpillars
on the dining room windowsill.

While Margaret cared for the wildlife,
she dreamed of becoming a scientist.
She dreamed of going off to the jungle.
She would travel. She would do
exciting and daring things—
things only a fearless woman would do.
It was a big dream for a young girl.
And Margaret was afraid of many things.
She was afraid of the dark.
She was afraid
of staying alone in the house.
How would she ever become fearless?

Minnie knew how to help.

She thought of games

that would help Margaret face her fears.

On moonlit nights,

Minnie raced her around the house.

Darkness soon became Margaret's friend.

Other nights, Minnie snuggled Margaret

into a chair with a favorite book.

Then she and Joseph left Margaret

alone in the house,

first for a few minutes,

later for a few hours.

Each day, Margaret took small steps

toward her dream.

Before long,

Margaret was ready to explore the world.

But she did not set off

to the tangled vines of the jungle.

As a young woman,

she found a new way to travel

when she began taking photos.

This change in interests happened

while Margaret was in college.

Her father died,

leaving the family without much money.

For Joseph,

taking pictures had been a hobby.

For Margaret,

it became a way to earn money.

She worked hard,

snapping pictures and selling them.

At times, she found herself

doing daring things to get pictures.

She climbed up a rope to a rooftop.

She crawled down a manhole

to a dark tunnel.

The camera made Margaret take risks,

and she enjoyed every scary moment.

It soon became clear—the camera

was her ticket to adventure.

After college, Margaret took her camera
and dashed off to Cleveland, Ohio.
There, at the age of 23,
she began her life's work.
It was the fall of 1927.
People were building
new factories everywhere.

In this city of clanging and clutter,
Margaret tried to capture
the beauty of things in motion.
There were bursts of steam,
chugging trains,
the rushing flow of fiery hot metal.
Margaret found beauty
where others did not.
But she faced problems.

When Margaret tried
to get into the steel mills,
the men there stopped her.
They thought she would faint
from the heat.
They could not understand
what beauty she could find
in dark buildings
full of sooty, shuddering machines.
But Margaret did not give up.
She was not afraid of the heat.
She knew she could find beauty
in the mills.

She talked to the owner of the steel mill.
She kept talking
until he let her take pictures.
Margaret amazed everyone
with her photos.
Through her eyes, machines were not
ugly hunks of metal.
They became artful shapes and curves,
alive with the glow of flying sparks.

By the 1930s, Margaret was gaining fame
and getting paid well for her work.
She was even getting chosen for jobs
before men.
But the 1930s were not a good time
for everyone in this country.
Many people lost their jobs.
The hungry and homeless
were everywhere.
Seeing this, artists and writers
made changes in their work.
They began to take an interest in people.
Along with others, Margaret chased after
the heartbreaking stories of the day.

In 1934, Margaret raced to the Midwest
to take pictures in the Dust Bowl states
for *Fortune* magazine.
There, she saw scorched, dried-up soil.
It had not rained there for several years.
The land was useless for growing crops.
The farmers were helpless.
When Margaret saw this suffering,
people suddenly became important to her.
She made a promise to herself.
She would try to understand people
and tell their stories in her pictures.

Her new interest in people
came at just the right time.
A magazine about people
was about to begin.
It was called *Life*.
It was a news magazine
with few words but lots of big pictures.
*Life* and Margaret seemed perfect
for each other.
Margaret was willing to risk her life
and travel anywhere.
*Life* gave her the chance to do this.

The editors of *Life* sent Margaret
on one adventure after another.
In January 1937, Margaret took pictures
of the terrible Louisville, Kentucky, flood.
She snatched rides in rowboats.
She hopped onto a large raft.
Nothing seemed to stop Margaret
from getting her pictures.

In fact, nothing meant more to Margaret
than getting her pictures.
It was not always easy for others
to work with her.
Margaret wanted things done quickly.
If a helper worked too slowly,
she sometimes pushed the person aside
and did the job herself.
Many workers at *Life* did not like her.
But Margaret always got great photos.
She thrilled at the challenge
of getting to a story first.
She did things
women had never done before.
Each day she faced new dangers.
Each day she became more fearless.

Margaret's most daring adventures
began overseas in the spring of 1941.
World War II was raging in Europe.
Germany had invaded several countries.
*Life's* editor, Wilson Hicks, was sure
that Germany would attack Russia next.
He sent Margaret packing.
On June 22,
a month after Margaret reached Russia,
German troops stormed
across the border.

Margaret waited in Moscow.

She was the only person there

from an outside country

who was ready to photograph the attack.

When bombing started there,

she would get the pictures.

She would let nothing stop her.

One evening, Margaret stayed
at the American government offices,
waiting for the nightly attack.
At ten o'clock, she heard the hum
of German planes on their way.
She went up to the roof.
Searchlights were sweeping the sky.
She watched their beams
cross and recross,
searching for the enemy.
The planes came closer.
Soon she could hear the roar overhead.

Bursts of color riddled the blackness.

Flashes of light rattled the night.

Margaret had seen bombing before,

but this was different.

Flares dropped from the planes

and floated down as blazing balls

of yellow, orange, and red.

Firebombs exploded on the ground,

sending flames shooting up into the air.

Russian machine guns shot back

with glowing bullets

streaking a bright red trail.

It was like the fireworks of a madman.

There was so much happening at once.

It was out of control.

The bombs were destroying buildings.

The bombs were killing people.

But Margaret did not think about this
while she was working.

She thought the bombing was beautiful.

She enjoyed the excitement.

With her helmet strapped tight,
Margaret went to her camera.

She pointed it toward
the most dazzling action.

She struggled to focus
by the light of the flares.

Then she uncapped the lens and waited.

The Germans bombed Moscow 22 times
before Margaret left in late September.
She photographed almost every attack.
Her pictures of the bombing let
Americans see
what Germany was doing in Europe.
In 1942, the United States joined
England, Russia, and the other countries
fighting to stop Germany.
In the summer of that year,
Margaret was sent to England as the first
American woman war reporter.
This time, her pictures would be used
by the United States Air Force
and *Life* magazine.

Margaret would now have the exciting job
of taking pictures of men in battle.
Margaret was thrilled
to be working for the Air Force.
She loved taking pictures from airplanes.
She begged to fly with the bombers.
But combat missions were dangerous—
too dangerous for a woman,
many people thought.
The Air Force sent men reporters instead.

But soon Margaret heard
about secret plans
for the next big battle.
England and America were going to
invade the coast of North Africa
and attack German forces there.
Margaret wanted to go along,
and the Air Force let her.
They sent her by sea.
The night before they reached Africa,
a torpedo struck Margaret's ship.

While the troops and nurses marched
to the lifeboats,
Margaret scrambled to the top deck
with one camera.
The ship might sink. Margaret might die.
But fear did not stop Margaret.
She was busy trying to work.
She glanced at the sky.
It was dark, but the moon was bright.
Was there enough light to take pictures?
Suddenly a voice called out
from the loudspeaker. "Abandon ship!"

No longer could Margaret hide
behind her camera.
She raced to a lifeboat,
afraid it might leave without her.
She had never been so terrified.
Later, in the lifeboat, thoughts of work
made Margaret forget her fears.
She thought of the great pictures
she wanted to take.

There were people swimming,
and people hanging on to floating rubble.
Margaret looked at the rope nets
hanging from the side of the ship.
Hundreds of people
were scrambling down,
trying to escape the sinking ship.
But Margaret could not take pictures
of this nightmare.
It was too dark for the film to work.

After floating on the sea for eight hours,
they were rescued by another ship.
As soon as Margaret landed in Africa,
she ran into General Jimmy Doolittle,
who had let her come with the troops.
"Maggie," he said, "do you still
want to go on a bombing mission?"
"Oh, you know I do," she gasped.
"Well, you've been torpedoed.
You might as well go through everything,"
said General Jimmy.
Then he phoned the 97th Bomb Group,
and Margaret flew to their secret base.

A chance to fly with the bombers!

Which mission would it be?

She hoped it would be a major battle.

On the morning of the mission,

Margaret sat with hundreds of airmen

among the ruined buildings of the village,

as officers uncovered the maps.

The mission—

destroy the El Aouina airfield in Tunis.

Margaret's wish had come true.

El Aouina was a major target, a place

where German troops were landing.

Margaret boarded the lead plane,

a B-17 loaded with bombs.

She was about to take part

in a mission of death.

But she gave little thought to that.

She might be killed.

But that idea did not stop her

from doing her job.

When they took off,

she began taking pictures

of the men at their posts.

As they neared the target,
Margaret squeezed herself
and her bulky camera
between the rows of bombs.
There she watched a crewman pull out
the safety pins from the bombs.
The pins kept the bombs from exploding.
Margaret did not stop to think
how scared the crewman might be.
Without a word, she snapped a picture.
When the camera's flash went off,
the crewman was frightened.
He thought the bombs were exploding
in his hands!

Soon the air attack began.

The bombers dropped their load.

The Germans shot back.

The bombers weaved and rolled.

They tried to dodge the shots.

Margaret's plane was hit twice,

but fear did not stop Margaret.

She took pictures at a breathless pace.

She wanted to record everything.

There were bombs bursting below,

fiery flashes darting up,

smoke rising from the ground.

Suddenly, German fighter planes

swooped down on them from the clouds.

The gunners exchanged fire.

Two of the U.S. bombers were shot down,

but Margaret's plane escaped.

As she shot pictures

of the airfield in flames,

she gave little thought

to the people on the ground.

Because she could not see the people,

Margaret, like others, found it easy

to forget about those who died.

But she faced that side of war

when she saw it from the ground.

Death pressed closer in Italy,

in a place called Purple Heart Valley.

There she joined the troops in the field.

In the middle of heavy fighting,

she took pictures from ditches.

For Margaret, this was worse

than the bombing of Moscow.

While German shells swooshed overhead

from one direction,

American gunfire streaked

from the other side.

Explosions shook the ground.

If Margaret got frightened here,

she could not run to a shelter.

She could only crouch deeper

into the earth.

At the Eleventh Field Hospital,
she stayed close to the front line
and again saw war up close.
The hospital was just a group of tents,
each bearing a painted-on red cross.
The Germans were only six miles away.
The night she arrived, a German shell
exploded only 30 feet from her tent.

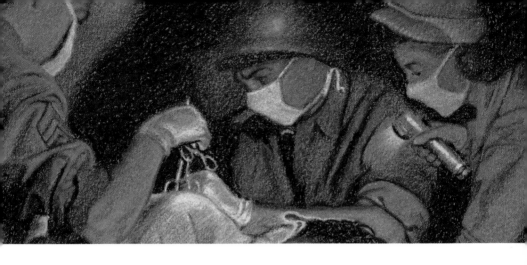

After the explosion,

Margaret went to the operating tent.

She found the doctors wearing helmets

and working by flashlight.

Margaret watched the wounded

being carried in.

She saw soldiers bleeding.

She heard them crying

for the pain to stop.

It was a sickening sight.

But Margaret stayed in the tent all night

and took pictures.

The world never saw those pictures.
They were lost in the mail.
But near the end of the war,
Margaret's photos helped the world learn
the truth about German death camps.
For years, men, women, and children
had been herded into boxcars
and sent to camps to be killed.
Many of these people were Jews.
Hitler, Germany's Nazi leader,
hated the Jewish people.
He blamed them for Germany's problems.
He wanted to see them all dead.

During the spring of 1945,
Margaret traveled with American troops
led by General Patton,
as they swarmed into Germany.
Germany was about to lose the war.
In April, the troops reached Buchenwald.
They went to free the prisoners
being held in the death camp there.

When Margaret and Patton's troops

reached Buchenwald,

what they found there shocked them.

There were so many dead,

and the people they found alive

were almost dead.

Margaret took pictures as if in a daze.

Her mind did not want to know

what her eyes were seeing.

There was no excitement for her now.

There was no thrill.

She took pictures of dying men

in their bunks.

She took pictures of men standing silently

behind a barbed wire fence.

Margaret's pictures in *Life* magazine

shocked the world.

Buchenwald was only one of the camps.
There were many others.
Hitler had millions of people killed.
While Margaret snapped pictures
throughout Germany,
she tried to piece together
the Nazi puzzle.
Surely most Germans
knew about the camps.
They had to know, thought Margaret.
How could they let this happen?

The war ended.

Margaret continued to travel.

She cared more about people

than she ever had before.

In each country, she searched out

people in trouble.

In 1946, *Life* sent Margaret to India.

In southern India, she explored

the leather-tanning factories,

where workers made

cowhides into leather.

The factories were
terrible places to work.
Tanning was done in large pits of acid.
When Margaret went in with her camera,
her eyes stung and teared.
At first, she could hardly see.
Then she spotted the children.
They were hopping up and down
in the pits,
pressing acid into the cowhides
with their feet.
Margaret felt sorry for these children.
They came from poor families,
and there were no laws to protect them.
But Margaret knew India was changing.
She hoped that new laws would bring
a better life for these children.

In 1949, *Life* sent Margaret
to another troubled part of the world—
South Africa.
There, she followed black Africans
into the gold mines,
two miles underground.
The mines were dark and hot.
While taking pictures,
Margaret started to feel sick.
She could hardly move or speak.
The person in charge quickly took her
to a cooler part of the mines.

Margaret knew she could not change
the way white people treated blacks
in South Africa.
But she hoped her pictures might help.
Her picture of two gold miners
was one of her most important
and treasured photos.
It showed the men with sweat pouring
down their bare chests and faces—
faces with sad eyes.

Sadness and suffering were not part
of Margaret's childhood dream.
As a young girl,
she looked at life as an adventure.
And when she became a woman,
the thrill of facing danger
drove her to succeed.
But along the way, Margaret found
a greater meaning to her work.
Her parents had given her a special gift
when she was young.
They taught her how to live her life
without being afraid.
In turn, Margaret gave a special gift
to the world.
Through her pictures, she gave the world
a chance to see and remember the truth.

# Afterword

Margaret Bourke-White was known not only for her photos, but also for the books she wrote and took pictures for, which tell of her experiences. She produced seven books on her own and three with her second husband, the writer Erskine Caldwell.

Margaret was married twice, but both marriages were brief and ended in divorce. She never had children. She met many people during her worldwide adventures. But she took little time to form close friendships. Her work was her life.

When Parkinson's disease struck her in 1951, Margaret faced the illness alone and with her usual courage. For almost 20 years, she fought (by exercising) to keep movement and control of her legs, arms, fingers, and speech.

She worked for *Life* until 1957. During the last seven years of her life, she wrote her autobiography, *Portrait of Myself*, at her home in Connecticut. Margaret Bourke-White died on August 27, 1971, at the age of 67.

# Important Dates

June 14, 1904—Margaret Bourke White born in New York City. She later made her middle name part of her last name, adding a hyphen between the two.

1906–1921—Grows up in Bound Brook, New Jersey, and graduates from Plainfield High School

1927—Begins work in Cleveland, Ohio, taking pictures of industry

1929—Begins working for *Fortune* magazine

1930—Becomes first person from outside Russia to take pictures of industry in that country

1934—Takes pictures of the Dust Bowl for *Fortune*

1936—Becomes one of the first four people to take pictures for *Life* magazine

1941—Takes pictures of German forces attacking Russia

Spring 1942—First woman to become war reporter to U.S. Air Force

December 1942—Her ship is torpedoed while heading toward North Africa

1943—First woman to fly on a U.S. bombing mission

1971—Died in Stamford Hospital, Stamford, Connecticut